Homeground

Homeground

A collection of poems by Brian Fereday.

Illustrations by Fiona Clucas

Inspired by the landscape
and people of South Westmorland

Published in 2015
© Copyright Fulmus Press

ISBN 978-0-9932143-0-1

Cover and Book Design by Russell Holden
www.pixeltweakspublications.com

Cover painting by Fiona Clucas
www.fiona-clucas.co.uk

Printed by Short Run Press Ltd, Exeter

All rights reserved without limiting the rights under copyright reserved above, no parts of this publication may be reproduced, stored in or introduced into a retrieval system, or transmitted in any form, or by any means (electronic, mechanical, photocopying, recording or otherwise) without the prior written permission of both the copyright owner and the publisher of this book.

FULMUS
PRESS
WWW.FULMUS.CO.UK

Acknowledgements

Thank you to all the following who have contributed in their own special way to the production of
'Homeground'

Russell Holden, Liz Nuttall, Andrew Forster

Sheila and Judy

Richard

The Witherslack Group of Artists & Makers

Virginia

Ursa and Sam

Sarah and Geoff

Fiona and Kit

Maureen and Arnold

Ros and David

Low Sizergh Barn

DJ and Jean

This book is dedicated to two people.

To Fiona, my wife, without whose constant support and vision this book would never have happened.

The other person is George, my Dad, who took me to woods and wild places and showed to me 'the Way'

Contents

Stirrings 1
Alert..1
Seasons..................................1
Cycles 2
Dewtime 2
Adaptation 4
Day Dreams...........................4
Impermanence.......................5
Green Man.............................6
Bliss..8
Cliff Edge 10
Return 11
Consequence 12
Gooseberry Picker................13
Soft Drink 15
Sun Shower..........................15
Welcome Visitors.................16
Wanderer 16
Oblivion 17
Supermarket, Kendal...........17
The Burden 18
Last Taties July 15th 2014 22
The Prophet 23
Jam Making 24
Garden Shed........................25
Late December dawn 26
Bounty..................................30
Attachment...........................31
The Seeker...........................32
The Season Compass..........33
Seen at Fishcarling Headland...34
Summertime........................36
The Crop 39
Night Sky 40
Refuge..................................41

Homesick..............................41
Arrival...................................42
Northern Tales 42
Food Chain...........................44
Impasse 46
Seadogs 47
Barley Birds 48
Airspace 49
H.M.S. Berlingo 51
Marsh Parade 52
Whinfell Moon 54
Earth and Sky.......................55
The Reply 57
Recycle 58
Orchard Basking..................58
The Longing 59
The Opportunist 60
Fey 61
Taken....................................62
Departure.............................64
Mother Earth........................65
Predator 67
Flock.....................................68
Round Earth.........................69
Old Haunt.............................70
Fantasy on an East wind 71
Paradise 72
Letting Go.............................74
Feeding Up 75
Curlew..................................77
Fluke.....................................77
Caretakers............................78
Encircled..............................79
Howe Lane...........................80
Faith......................................81

Adventurer 81
Hampsfell, Winter 2013............82
Venus...83
Oak Mother 84
Late Flowering 86
Where The Clouds Go 87
Fellside Cottage Orchard..........88
Infatuation 90
Morning incident.......................92
Ward 17.......................................93
Midsummer's Day 94
Roadkill Oystercatcher 96
Limestone Scar...........................97
Morning Star 98
Impending Storm 99
Quarry Wood Quartet 100
Unforgettable 102
Performance 103
Meltdown..................................104
Cuckoo Pint..............................105
Herb Paris 105
Red Berry Folds 106
Fullsome 107
October Gather........................108
Clump 108
King Of The Woods.................109
Portal...110
Whitbarrow February..............112
Wall – gapping 114
Estuary 116
November Quartet 119
Before the storm 120
December Duo.........................121
Voices 122

March 124
Tide..125
Plough 127
Flow...128
Dissolving Land. 130
After the shower 131
September.................................133
Messages 134
Fulfilment 135
Walking the Marsh Road.........136
Snowy Anthills.........................137
Attitude 138
Moss Road 139
Old Road – October................140
Christmas Time 141
Life Support..............................142
July, Sizergh Fell.......................143
Plain Road 144
Living with the Artist...............146
Out of season 148
Travellers...................................148
Illumination 148
Whitbarrow gift 149
Summer's End 150

Foreword

What does it mean to be at home in a place? For poets there is a long tradition of writing your way into a place. It's hard to go anywhere in the Central Lakes without encountering Wordsworth's poems, and more recently we might think of George Mackay Brown and Orkney. Their responses to the places they find themselves in shape the way we see the landscape.

Brian Fereday has lived in Westmorland all his life, entering into the landscape for work and pleasure, and for around fifteen years he has been responding to that landscape through poetry. It's a poetry of locality: Sizergh Fell, Whinfell, Heversham Marsh and Fishcarling Headland are among the settings for minutely-detailed sketches of a life lived alongside nature. They record encounters with hares, pike, crows, starlings, spiders; they note walks on fells and marshes and old roads; and they note the changes as the seasonal cycle continues. Sometimes the landscape prompts memories, both sweetly nostalgic or things to battle with. All this adds up to answer the question of what it means to be on Homeground. In a particularly moving poem, the familiar landscape of Westmorland is sensed from a hospital ward in a different town, as the author is filled with longing to be back.

The poems are accompanied by Fiona Clucas' images, which have the same alertness to a landscape in flux, constantly shifting.

Above all, these poems celebrate. They are moments of attention to things that too often pass us by.

Andrew Forster
Poet and Literature Officer

The Homeground

South Westmorland

Introduction

The poems stem from a lifetime of observing and working on the land. Sometimes past, sometimes present and mixed styles. They come from a love of the place and a need from the author to touch hearts and break down barriers between man and nature.

Brian Fereday was born in Levens in 1950. From an early age he worked in gardens growing vegetables and in the woods helping 'older fellas'. As a young boy he explored his local woods, mosses, fells and the estuary learning about landforms, the seasons, fauna and flora. As a young man he worked as a woodland research scientific assistant and then for a local forestry contractor.

For the next thirty-eight years he worked for *The National Trust* at Sizergh as a forester and estate manager.

Since taking early retirement he has continued his interest and involvement in the regeneration and conservation of local woodland and orchards; benefiting wildlife and humans alike.

Brian has quietly been writing poetry for fifteen years and has only more recently brought his prose out to share with us and pass on his passion for his surroundings in this native county of South Westmorland.

Brian's wife Fiona Clucas has lived in Cumbria for twenty years. Her inspiration also comes from her love of the many varied habitats in this area; its wildlife, flora, the elements and their effects on the landscape. She is a member of *The Society of Wildlife Art* and *The lake Artists Society*.

Stirrings

Summer evening stillness.

A branch twitches,

A brown bird appears.

Alert

Raindrops on the shed roof.

Then somewhere a dog barks.

Seasons

A summer rainstorm,

Turns to a snowstorm of petals.

Cycles

Watching raindrops

Make leopardskin forms on dry flagstones.

Water earthed once more.

Lightning flashes.

Creation announced

With a drumroll of thunder.

Dewtime

Moths rising and bats hunting,

Dusky earthy stillness.

White roses make pale faces,

Watching from the dark corner.

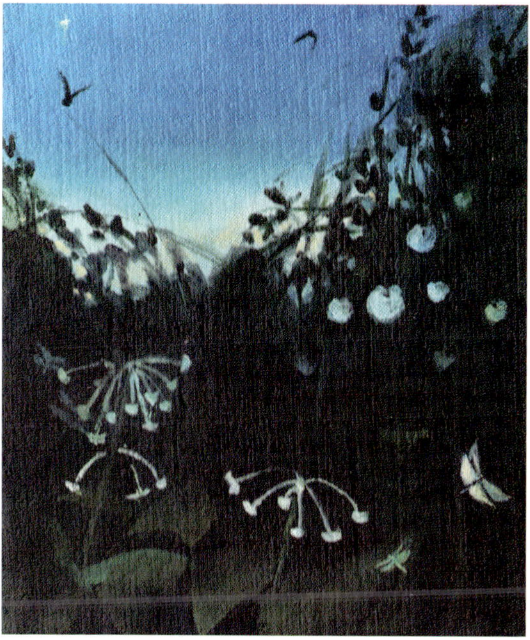

Adaptation

After the storm,

Snails on paths.

Day Dreams

Prompted by a warm sunburst,

I sow the Calendula seeds.

Imaginings of August days,

Orange faces looking up to the sun.

Impermanence

Raindrops falling on windowsill, explode,

Like the sprawl of spider's legs.

A rose leaf bears up under a constant methodical drip,

Singled out it prevails,

A breath of air and a rush of rainwater,

Spider shapes flash momentarily,

Then absorbed,

By a growing pool of water.

Green Man

If this garden was ever ours,

I sense it no longer is.

I know this,

It's over in the wooded corner.

Sit by it's edge,

Only a few square feet,

Denser than the wildwood.

Bush, bramble, tree,

No, it's not the vegetation.

There's something in there,

Sit and feel the watcher's presence.

Look carefully,

Nothing to see,

Or is there.

There's always an eye returning your gaze.

A minute spark of light reflected back.

Search, shapes loom out the greenness.

Not always the same shape,

Sometimes two.

So still, silent and secretive.

Look all you want,

There's no movement.

If you look away the shape has gone.

Only an arm's length away,

Though further than this.

I am outside the magic,

However much I wanted to enter,

If I did the spell would break.

Something has come home to that corner,

Returned to that small patch of ground.

It can't be described or named,

I cry with sadness and joy.

Bliss

Droning insects of summertime,

Soaking up potent summer energy.

Warm soil brings perfumed connection,

Sundrawn essences from leaf and flower.

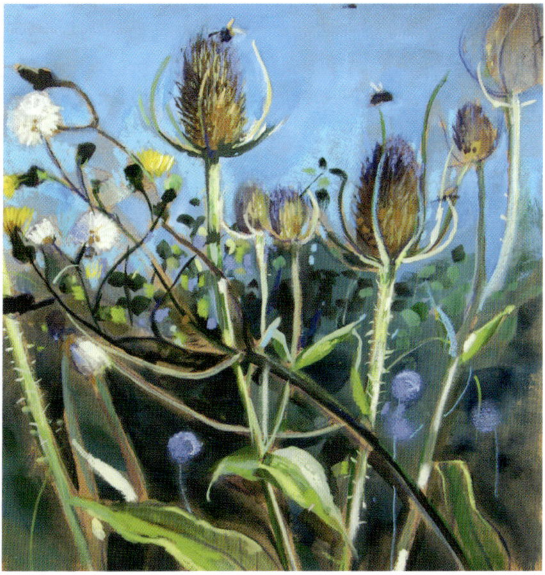

Cliff Edge

Sunlight fills the room,

Spider stitches ceiling to wall.

Flicking sensitive legs,

Seeking nuances of texture.

Smoothness and a fall,

Now suspended,

On the airy face of the wall.

In complete presence.

The climb back begins,

Suspended over the bedroom's abyss.

Sensitive legwork,

Leading back to the ceiling's moonscape.

Return

Arrived from the dry banks of violets,

Driven here by the west wind.

Faded colours, ragged wings,

Tell of a life passing.

Buddleia flowers, rich and cultured,

Oozing liquid perfume.

Insect elixir flows.

Unblinking crystalline eyes,

Tongue probes deep and long.

Drunken bees for company.

She takes a draught of nectar.

Wings angling towards the sun,

She sways on the flowerhead.

In a butterfly paradise,

Until the next storm takes her.

Consequence

Still July evening,

A fading rose crumbles.

Falling to release another score

Of perfumed petals.

Gooseberry Picker

Beneath these leaves is another world.

A forest of green stem and leaf.

Herbs drawn by the light,

Pushing through prickly confines.

Shafts of sunlight penetrate the deep,

Revealing bright suspended jewels

Under the vaulted roof.

Of soft leaf and woody branch.

She defends her treasure,

Nettles and thorns lurk here.

Gems are stolen in greedy handfuls,

Carried away by the thief.

Green canopy above,

On hands and knees I seek.

Skin torn and nettled.

I am the thief.

The picker of gooseberries!

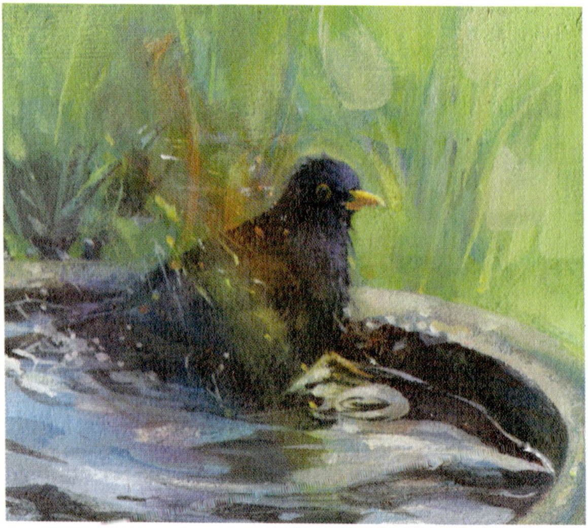

Soft Drink

Still July evening,

Blackbird comes,

Sips water,

Shatters the mirror,

With gentleness.

Sun Shower

Blackbird takes a bath

In the sunlight.

I watch as the water droplets,

Envelop him in a rainbow.

Welcome Visitors

Hot July day,

In this man made desert.

Cleg lands,

On my neck,

Realisation,

We've got it right.

Wanderer

Village garden,

Cleg on my hand.

Lifted here,

By the warm wind.

A traveller from the moss.

Oblivion

July heat,

Drunken bees

on limeflowers,

Rocked by

A breeze of change.

Supermarket, Kendal

All out on this

July evening.

Bees and humans alike,

Gathering.

The Burden

Sitting here with the past

Tools and useful bits

Gathered around me.

From old men, all gone now.

Grandfathers, Fathers and friends

Tools, boards, bottles.

Some useful, some nostalgia

Kindlers of memory.

I look around me

Instantly a story,

An image from the past appears

I see hands working tools,

Spades, hammers, spanners, axes.

And there's that bit of wood

That so and so gave me.

That old coat that used to be ------.

I see hands through different eyes.

Through the wonderment of child's eyes,

Through young man's eyes

Envying skill and knowledge.

Through sad eyes,

Conscious of men's waning powers.

Then I'm drawn to my own hands

Have others thought that of me.

Who will take on this store of the past.

Who would want such

In these plastic, electronic, disposable times

I sit in the sun and muse,

In the doorway to past lives.

Honeysuckle and bramble have worked
Themselves within this place
As if interested in my past.
Spiders and bees visit here
And stay sometimes, to them,
The shed, a cave or hollow tree.

Sometimes I can't abide
In this place.
Melancholy for a golden age
Takes me.
The inner sanctum is where
The altar of memories resides.

Don't approach unless prepared

The spectres of thought

Are always waiting.

Waiting for the unwary,

Before I realise

I could be back in 1957.

Who will think of my hands

Remember which were my

Work tools.

Will they confuse them

With some other faded life

Who has a piece

In the collection.

Meanwhile on this

Summer's evening

The blackbirds feed

Their young in the ivy.

The dog sleeps in the sun

Until a sound from an open window

A crying baby.

Already fearful.

Last Taties July 15ᵀᴴ 2014

Last root, July 21.

Deep under heavy top

Fork – steel tines

Hunger for tuber flesh

Lever and there they are

White skins, dusting

Of dry, summer soil.

Last root, sadness now

Rain will fall

Wind will roar

Land will freeze

Snow will melt

Seasons will turn

Before we dig again.

The Prophet

July, cloudless sky

High raven

Circles the village

A black speck

In the blue

Makes announcements and predictions

Is there anyone

Listening down there

Makes another circle

Disappears to the north.

Raven has gone

I still hear the wild voice

Delivering stories

Of rivers, rock, gales and rain.

And here I am, potting plants.

But I store the calls

In my heart.

Jam Making

Picking, Joy, Laughter,

Earth, Yield, Bounty,

Sweet, Orange, Red,

Skins, Ripe, Transparent,

Warmth, Smells, Food,

Jars, Bottles, Labels,

Fire, Stove, Shelves,

Boiling, Wrinkling, Settings,

Pride, Frustration, Excitement,

Heart, Giving, Love.

Garden Shed

Hoverflies and white roses

Fig leaves and shoots from the vine

Makes dark inside the shed.

Honeysuckle fronds fall

limply across the bench,

Confused between light

From door and window.

Green reflection of leaves and

shoots in a setting sun.

Makes a mellow blend of plant and light.

In the darkest recesses

Lies the insect realm

There are those unaware of the danger,

Then down the silken tunnel

rushes the spider

To claim her prize.

Late December dawn

Viewed from the window

In this, wild, woody garden

Faint movements in the almost dark.

Shapes, large and small, stirring,

Halting, advancing

Both treeborne and grounded.

Shed is dusted white.

Leaves of Autumn,

Crisped and curled

Ragged edges of frost crystals

Visible as the sun draws near.

Now the dark shapes

Manifest as birds.

Birds, searching for sustenance,

Frantically, on this icy morning.

I watch as the sun

Lights up the tallest treetop

As colour imbues.

A blackbird surveys the scene

Looking down on it's kin

As they scour the ground.

Small birds flit.

Ground to branch,

Plant to plant,

Ground to either.

The Flock moving across the garden,

Nothing escaping attention.

Squabbling, on seed feeder.

Hanging by toe ends,

Whirring wings, maintain position,

Titmouse, sparrow, spinks, green linnet.

In the rush for food

After the night of frost.

I wonder where they sleep.
Feet curled over an icy branch
Or a hole in a wall.
Cold stone surrounding.
Mindful of the cat in the dark.
Sharp teeth on a winter's night
Turn to a bundle of feathers
In the morning light.

Sunlight extending
Unabated they come.
Goldfinches now,
On golden teazles
Probing, prising, fluttering.
Above emptying seedheads
They hover,
Light and colourful
As blown autumn leaves.

The crow family arrive

Heads go down

As the raiders rule.

Beakfuls of food

Flung over shoulders,

Scattered on the earth

By black, shiny toes.

Leaving as quickly

As they came

As if to some corvine signal.

Unknown to all but them.

The Flock returns,

Jackdaw visit over, life resumes.

Meanwhile the wren, unconcerned

With the lives of others.

Hunts for spiders in the wall,

Small brown body,

Beady eyes and needle beak

Forever seeking.

Bounty

The tatie field burgeons

Frost a legend now.

White flower and swelling tuber.

Rich green rows on the Marsh.

Secret paths for the travelling hare.

Attachment

Green, water woman's tresses

Ungroomable, washed by the crystal flow.

Wild, loose, unkempt.

Tossed by the water's breeze.

A skimming swallow passes low

Over the waving locks.

For an instant, a trailing wing,

Strokes her floating hair.

The Seeker

Calm May morning and an early sun.

White frost in the shadows,

Green growth curled and shocked.

Limp sap laden stems fallen.

Through the Fell gate

All is dry and bristly here

Accepting of the cold.

Over the bank, then,

Where the rising sun as melted frost,

Passing by, I glance sideways,

Unmoved by dog or man,

A brown, horned, cosmic cow,

Salutes the rising sun.

The Season Compass

Stood here beneath grey skinned trees.

I turn to the east to the promise of Spring.
Morning light, gifts, renewal and swallows return.

South, growing and summer, flowers, swelling fruits and warm sun.

West, I sense the harvest and return to the soil,
Rain and westerlies from the Great Ocean.

North, I feel the Winter cold, frost, snow,
And wild geese on a thin wind.

Sunrise over, I step out of the circle of stone.

Seen at Fishcarling Headland Winter 2013

Four mysteries over Fishcarling,

A shamanic dance in flight,

Enacting the unknown.

Rise and fall on the west wind,

Black feathered cloaks fluttering

Coarse shouts across the fields.

I see the hunter speeding in from the north.

Dark and swift, low over fields and hedges,

Arrow straight towards the host.

Ravens veer, climb and swoop,
Peregrine climbs higher, they follow,
Plunging clinging close to the assailant.

The ritual continues, changed now,
An expectant edge has arisen,
Drama constantly re-enacting.

Winding and unwinding,
Slowly disappearing over the sands,
As if bound together by a spell forever.

Summertime, Heversham Marsh

Herbage yields gently

Harmless breeze on the Marsh.

Yellowing seedheads, plumes of meadowsweet,

Perfumes of high summer.

Hedges sigh and whisper,

Filtering goodness from the wind

Leaves toy contentedly with light,

All shades of green.

Swallows rising on the wind,

Rejoice at the sun.

Denizens of the deep hedge,

Perch warily on exposed branches.

A man with a dog.

Senses warmth on his face,

Inhales the sea travelled air,

Returns the contented grin from his companion.

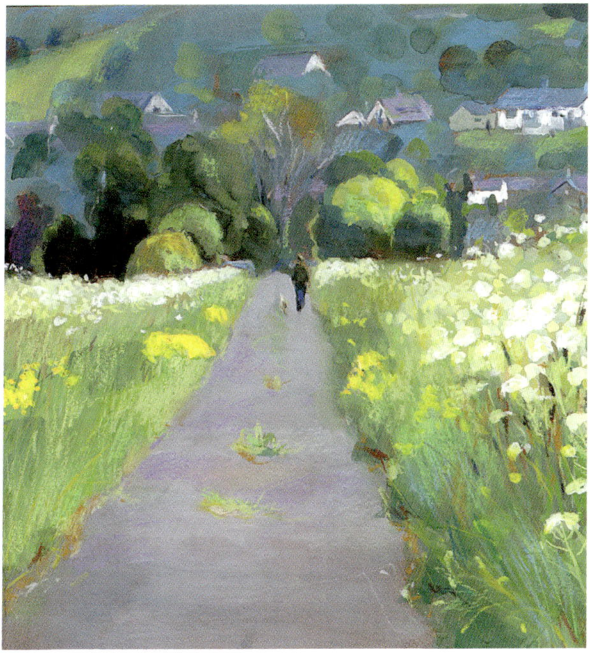

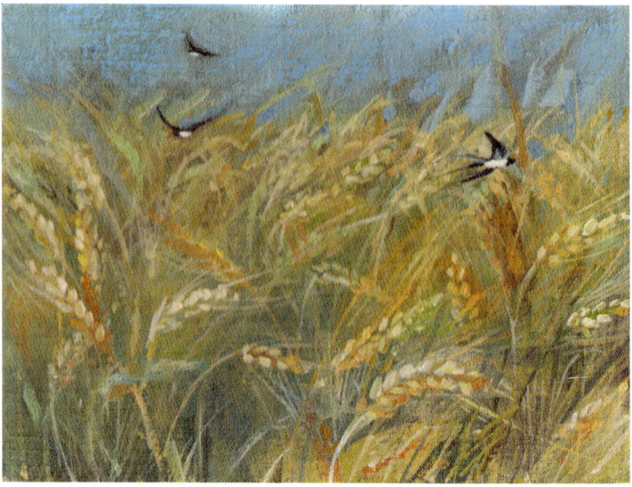

The Crop

Swell on the barley sea

Raised by the Marsh wind.

Swallows rise over breaking crests,

Flicking wings on greeting the breeze.

Whiskered seedheads wobble,

Antennae sifting the air.

Grain stalks filling under summer sun.

Soon the green tide will ebb

Leaving golden sands.

Night Sky

Sunset, August.

Overhead in the gathering blue

Stars are fashioned.

Refuge

Here behind this high hedge

Sheltered by leaf and stick

The east wind is breathless.

Homesick

A woman with two dogs.

Looking wistfully at the cornfield

Talks of her Lincolnshire home.

Arrival

On a clear, still October morning

I hear them.

Searching for the first sighting

Homing in on the calls.

Then, there they are extended across the sky,

High overhead,

I cry, not knowing why.

Northern Tales

October, still, clear morning

Calls from the north.

Far then near,

Carried on high level winds.

Now overhead in measured flight,

In constant converse.

Sharing stories of the summer passed.

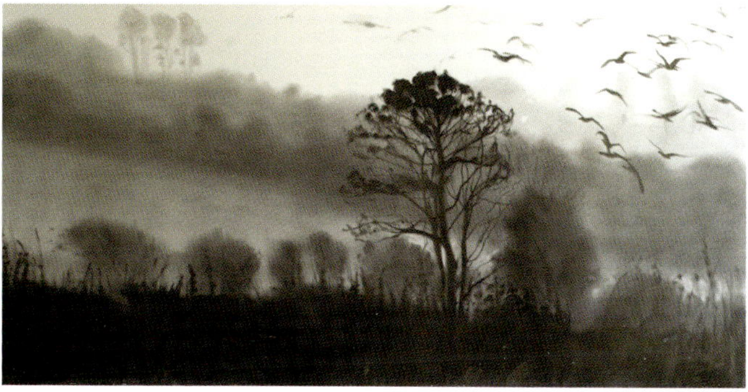

Food Chain

Westerly breeze off the Bay.

Rushing through the old oaks.

Hard, weather worn leaves

Making harsh sounds

Returning to earth.

After summer sun and storm.

Downwind an invisible stream issues.

A stream of insects.

Plucked from leaf and branch

In the moving air

Whisked off their refuge into space.

An assembly of swallows

Feed in the stream.

Stalling with each prey item

Wings quivering, holding position,

Then on into the wind.

Pass upon pass.

Open beaks, a communal net

Sweeping the air currents

For midge, fly or beetle.

With calls of encouragement

I stand beneath them.

Wishing them safe passage.

As vulnerable as insects themselves

In wind and airy space.

Impasse

A battered wooden gate

Held by a tight, rusted chain

Nettle and bramble

Imprison it's hangings.

Beyond the gate

An orchard draws me.

Young trees scarred by sheep teeth

Tangles of wood, wire and plastic.

Sheep look back at me

We weigh each other up,

Seadogs

Big gull overhead

Tack left, tack right

Rise and fall

On this lumpy westerly.

Dark against a dark sky,

Others follow in the gathering

No formation, no sequence.

As random as the wind.

Out to the banks

Exposed, tide scoured territory.

Roosting with beaks to the wind

Sometimes a blink of a yellow eye.

Barley Birds

Boisterous September westerly

Three crows flap out of the barley

Beneath them rises a swelling cloud

Of blue woodpigeons.

Airspace

Two ravens stalling in the wind

Over a field of red-gold barley.

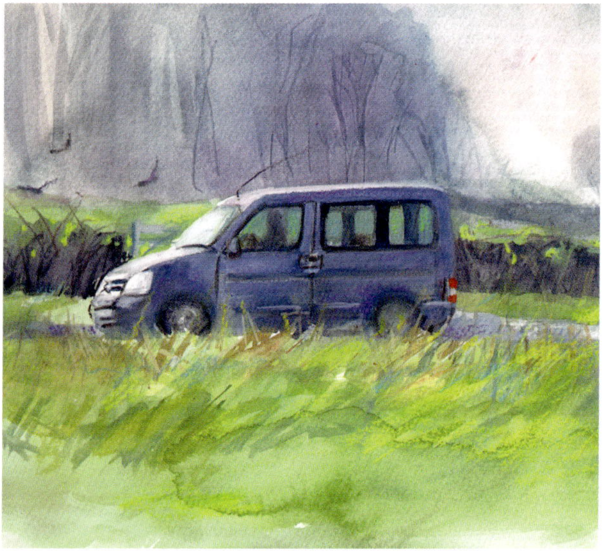

H.M.S. Berlingo

Steady at twenty miles per hour.
This old Marsh Road is a seatrack
No need to cross the floodbank
Sailing here on the rise and fall.

Fair day and a stiff east wind
Rattles and playfully gives us a push.
Four wheels hold firm as we lift and fall
Into and out of the wave troughs.

Foaming billows on either side
Cow Parsley tossed by the wind.
A headwind on turning to port
Ride the big wave over the stone bridge.

On we plunge, land in sight
We beach up the lane.
Looking down the swayback road
Setting sun and the Cow Parsley waves are red and gold.

Marsh Parade

Late afternoon,

On the distant floodbank

A line of milk cows, heading farmwards

Mixed shapes against soft light.

Humbacked veterans

Chopped steps, dragging feet, heads bowed.

Level backed young,

Full trot floating feet, ears pricked.

A skylark rises, bursts into song

Above our heads

Beak pointing to the sky

Disappears into the blue.

Back on the bank the march continues

Stragglers now, stiff legs, arched backs

Sad grotesque shapes against the horizon.

The last one kicks out as a sidling

cowdog nips her heel.

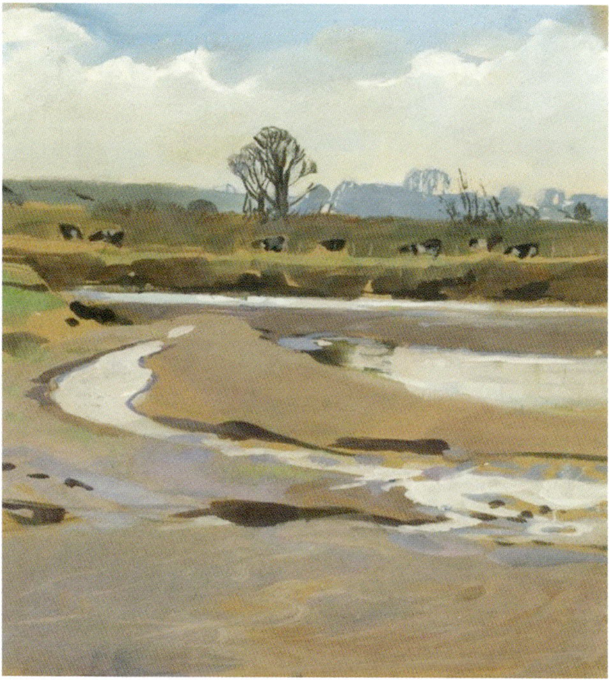

Whinfell Moon

Hoar frost tonight

On that curved hilltop

A resting flock watches.

Then, over the rim of the fell

A cloud glows with the rising moon

Deep blue shadows form.

The land soaks up the light

Looking down on the flock

The moon sees it's reflection

In a hundred soft eyes.

Return from Agnes Gill. September 2012.

Earth and Sky

A boiling cloud freed of the mountains

Watch it expand over the open mosses.

Flat black underbelly opens

Tendrils of hail strike earthwards.

An explosion of sunlight turns ice to gold

Foulshaw's woods become a back lit silhouette.

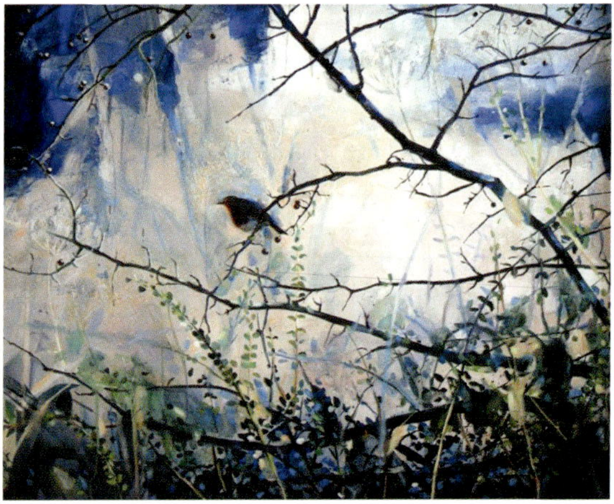

The Reply

Far moss in a grey light

A harsh crow call from the wood

There, in the mist,

Balancing on a tree top

Out of the deep hedge

A Robin sings four wistful notes.

Recycle

Far moss cast in a pewter light.

Here under the leaning oak

Raindrops rattle onto fallen leaves

Melding shiny, yellow leaf skins

Into air and soil.

Orchard Basking

Spring sunshine,

The east wind has fallen

To the faintest cool breath

Against my fingers.

As it flickers over the wall top.

The Longing

Raven slips over the hill

A bitter east wind assisting.

Sideways twist on sighting human form.

A companion rises from the dark trees

Wings flick in recognition

Gurgles and coughs as they join

Then over the wood to the west.

I imagine their deep, dark eyes

Perhaps a blink of pale eyelid

Flashing across the orb.

Minute lashes meshing momentarily

As an ice grain strikes from the air

I feel their vulnerability, tenderness arises.

I want to see the world through those eyes.

Then if the ice struck me

In a blink all would be well

Unconcerned, flying beyond the dark woods

Over sunlit limestone.

The Opportunist

April morning

White clouds on an easterly breeze.

Rise and fall of warmth

As the sun comes and goes.

When the cloud has passed

Feels good to have the sun on your back.

Fey

Moss top in front.

Bleached grass and heather sprigs

Swept flat at the whim of the wind.

The air is cold and dry, some say invigorating.

Feels more like

The final gesture from a long winter.

Taken

Stepping over the broken wall,

Over the boundary

Into the Place of Memories.

Another Spring

The past rises, life's stories glow.

Predictably the ghosts emerge.

Spectres of the living and the dead.

Nothing to fear in this gathering place

Only loss and grief to overcome.

We arrive here, the past and I often unexpectedly.

Drawn by something

Branch snap, leaf, bird, animal

Shade or shelter.

They like to meet me here.

The chosen battleground.

Finding their places

In random niches of recollection.

Time to withdraw from the conflict.

Some encounters, I win, some I lose.

I toss another coin into the spring

Creating a story for someone.

Tempting but can't stay here too long.

Out through the gate and the present appears.

Departure

Close the gate and shut the door

We don't belong here any more.

Mother Earth

Place of Memories again.

Green light surrounds

Each day and the Presence thickens.

Shoots like fingers worm through the soil

Reaching for the light of life and furtherance.

Leaf canopy is closing

Time runs short.

The world is closing in.

Otherworldly birdsong praises the true God.

Presence and form multiplies everywhere,

Piercing, protruding, forcing, uncurling,

Unfurling, bursting, cracking, lifting, --------.

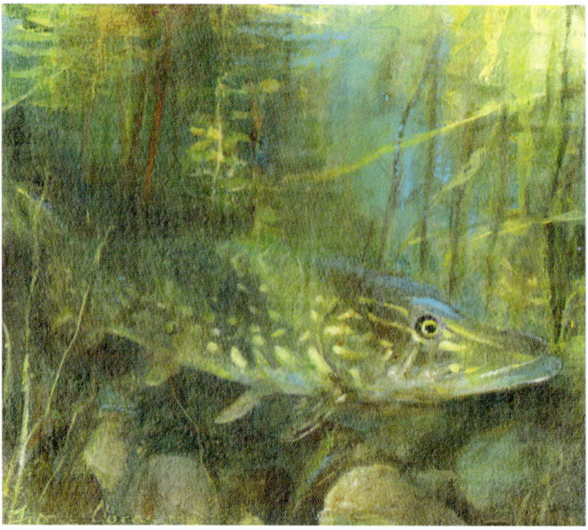

Predator

Pike under the bank.

Wayswharf.

Where the dub is three cart ropes deep.

Or so the old ones say.

Pike idling in slack water.

Sunlight dappling shining scales

Faintest movements of fin and tail.

Body honed for speed.

Pike caught unawares

Sensing an outline through the watery medium

Thought I caught a baleful glance

Just before that twist of body.

Pike tail flicks

Skin colour extinguished by the dark watermass.

Diving steeply, swiftly, our meeting over

Into the dub that's three cart ropes deep.

Flock

The low winter sun

Gives no respite for the eyes.

Across the rising ground a diffused glare

Conceals rock and tree.

Suddenly through narrowed vision

I see a movement.

A Fieldfare flock,

Each bird haloed in red and gold

Hard wing feathers flashing.

Round Earth

First hard frost of the winter.

Cobalt blue sky rising from the east.

I scan the hard Pennine horizon

As the world turns.

Barbon Fell falls over the edge.

We are dragged along uncontrollably

Plunging without fear.

We wait to meet the sun.

Old Haunt

Two Sundays to Christmas.

Wind backing to the north east.

Here on the Marsh again

Sunset has passed.

Fantasy on an East Wind

Breath of a running wolf,

Wolf breath from the Urals.

Paradise

High summer pasture.

A waft of air and Harebells ring.

Hare opens one wild, brown eye

Hears a melody long forgotten by us.

Reassured, the wild eye closes.

Hare blissful in the sun

On a couch of wild thyme

As the field of flowers begins to sing.

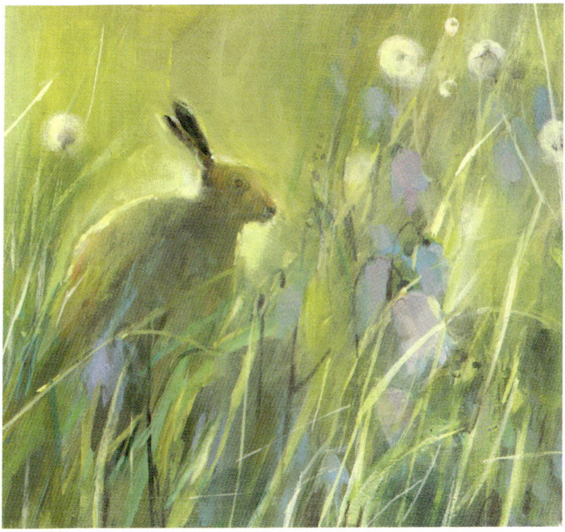

Letting Go

Out on the far moss tonight.

Wet fields and clay stained sheep.

A single soft animal presence

Lying here under the hedge.

I'm beyond recognition already.

Fast coming breaths, controlling

Holding, yet gradually

Releasing life before my eyes.

I turn away as another rain squall strikes.

Feeding Up

September beck side.

Above the tree line, flying clouds

And swirling martins.

Below the trees, swallows swarming

Over the rushing brown water.

Back edge of the storm

An easterly buffets the gathering.

Apparently fragile, feathered forms.

Their chatter holds no dread of the coming journey.

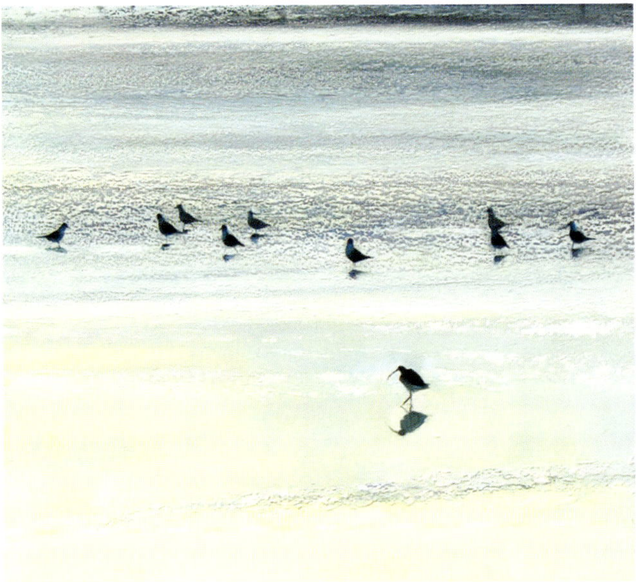

Curlew

Early September.

Dusk on the Marsh.

The softest breeze slides over my skin

Carrying Curlew calls from the sands.

I picture them, curved beaks probing the mud

Their song tell us sagas of the Bay.

Fluke

Flukes in the channel

Brown backed, pearl bellied slices

Finned limpets swept by the tide.

Caretakers

There is a dearth on the land

The summer cattle are gone.

Only rain filled footings remain

Where beasts tore at the season's grass.

Crows scour the ground

Where yesterday, lay the herd.

A shaft of sunlight

Lights the middle ground

In a watery hoofprint

A Rook sees itself in a golden light.

Encircled

Snow glare to the east

Crystal dust blows over us

The white creeps ever nearer

We, encircled on this land by the bay

These low hills our guardians

Take the weather as we watch.

Howe Lane

Water on chiggled steps

Water bursting from the ground

Following ancient streams

Alder and willow.

Faith

Two walkers study a map.

From the top of the wall

A small fly takes off into the unknown.

Adventurer

Snow lies on the yews

Up on that ridge

A small fly takes off into oblivion.

Hampsfell, Winter 2013

Over the cold grey shoulder the north-east wind began to sweep the clouds in streaks of blue-grey.
The mountains, floured with a riming of fresh snow seemed to brace themselves.
Trying to hide under a veil of soft, moist air they drew a blanket over themselves to cushion the cold blast.

Meanwhile over the bay the south-west quarter was filling with dark, murky cloud, a sky full of warm rain.
They were meeting where I was sat on top of this puddled, water washed fell.

The limestone I was sat on was deeply cold and the rainwater of the past months seemed to have penetrated far into it's water borne beginnings.

Venus

As they walked along the Marsh Road dusk had begun to gather. The way beyond was fading into the darkness but to the south-west the sky was clear and glowing with the parting sun. He looked to the left where a wren was angrily burying itself into the thickest part of the hedge for the night. When he looked up again the planet Venus had appeared. She had reappeared without warning and his mind slipped back to other November evenings.

November dusk

The way fades before us

Venus appears in the south-west

Above the glowing horizon.

Oak Mother

White frost on a late November morning

The moss fields are bitter places.

Water still lying, lurking in the grass

No place for sheep to lie or complain.

There is a place of

sanctuary though.

The rough branched oak has kept her leaves

She holds out her arms.

Green grass beneath her

Floating high on the moss

A root raft on the water

Green island on a

sparkling, frozen sea.

Sheep are beneath her

As chickens under a mother hen

When the sun strikes her branches

More of her brown leaves will fall.

The flock endures

As each day

The tree fold fades.

Late Flowering

October, after a storm

Cloud rift opens over the Sands

A dazzling sun shaft blinds

Through the glare a single, brilliant meadowsweet spray

Standing defiant yet vulnerable

The bloom beckons, but it's late

There are no insects to attract.

I stop to sniff

Drawn like a bee to the creamy, white bloom

In an instant summer returns

I stand to look at the sky

The cloud break has closed, sun hidden

As the next front comes off the bay

I walk on.

Looking back I see the flower waving

Madly in the wind.

Where The Clouds Go

Eyes raised to a limestone horizon

Where knife edged Yews cleave the wind

Crows wheel, wings flailing

Then effort over, they float

Carried away, east, where the clouds go.

Here in the trees below

Spring growth, sap and green

All rooted in deep earth

Woven into the thrush's song.

Fellside Cottage Orchard

Heady apple blossom perfume

Woody arms, offering charms

To the honey bees.

From the wood, they are drawn

Dark clamour

Around the hive.

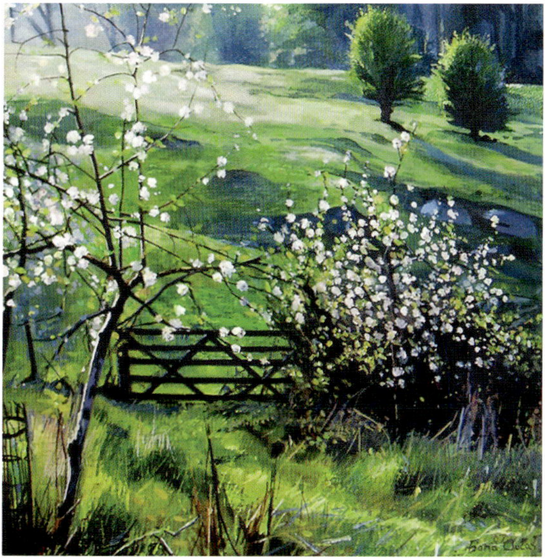

Infatuation

Beautiful chaos here.

I love you Westmorland orchards

Trees there

Form full and formless

Damson, apple, plum

Touched by senescence

Or the bright flush of youth.

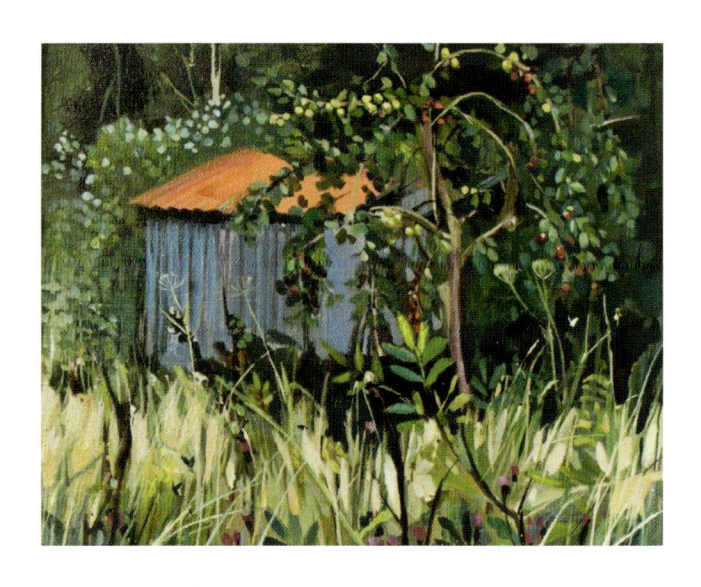

Nameless varieties

Favourite varieties

Sources of fruit and firewood

Where sheep may safely graze

Amongst blossom as white as lambswool.

Goldfinch nests on swaying branches

Crows on sweetest fruit.

Hedges, walls and fences

As diverse as the people

From generations past and present

Respect for human endeavour

Working the land.

Asking the unanswerable question

What to do with the big tree

That one "that never has anything on it"

Let her remain.

Morning incident

Dreamy, soft billed crow

Unskilled in corvine craft

Peers down at me

From a moss oak.

Chittering from the thorn

A bristling wren

Judgement clouded by ancestral memory

Sends us both on our way.

Ward 17 Hospital, Preston. June 2014

Night breeze lifts the blinds

My window is free

Breeze from the fields

And mosses of the Lancashire Plain

Having crossed the land to the north

The land I hold dear.

In this closed space of problems

That breeze is a welcome friend.

Come breeze a little more

But not to alert

The already alert carers.

As I whisper, the breeze

Responds with an extra push

Into the hot room

Sacrificing itself,

Casting itself into the breach

Curlew and cow breath

I relish its flavour

As it enters by the window.

Midsummer's Day

Midsummer's Day, the Marsh

Perfume of haygrass

Foaming meadowsweet

High grass.

Waving seed heads

Swaying hedges

Dog rose pink

Among shades of green.

Bubbling Curlews

Plaintive yet celebrative

Sea Pies agitated

Calling from the salt sand.

All enmeshed

By the wind

Whispering it comes

Over the flood bank.

Along ploughed furrows

Flexing fields of oats

Caressing all life

For now, in nurturing mood.

Roadkill Oystercatcher

Rachel told me.

Related her despair

Seeing the Sea Pie

Flat, lifeless

Body imprinted

Into roadstone and tar.

"Even worse" she said

Was seeing the mate

Standing,waiting alongside

Wanting for the other to fly.

Back to the fields

Back to the beck

When she returned

Both birds had gone

Didn't you know

They mate for life.

Limestone Scar

Wind curls around

This cliff edge

Flattened grasses

Remains of last summer's sweetness

Sheep have scoured the place

Nipped new shoots

First Spring green

Taken by eager mouths.

Morning Star

Lying here

A morning star

Out there, who knows where.

No glimmer of dawn

On this January morning.

Just the window frame

And the star.

So bright it is, just outside

But try to reach out to it.

Impending Storm

Morning, blue sky space

Flattened against the eastern horizon

By the latest storm out of Labrador.

A stir of wind from the sands

Rocking hedgerow thorns

Sighing through the oak tree.

Formless air, except for bird calls and salt grains

The empty mass

Pressed harder by the closing storm.

Still way west of Ireland

Yet near enough

To shroud the hilltops in cloud.

Quarry Wood Quartet

A straggly grass stem

Restless in the wind

Pecking at bare branches

With it's leaf beak.

Red – gold presence

Under the Yew

Bark and needle

The lowering sun

Is the painter.

A woodland clearing

Ten – thousand bees

Washed by a stream

Of sunlight.

Four Oaks and a Yew

In this safe circle

I've often sat

Seeking what ?

Unforgettable

Air falling from the fell

Filtered through a myriad of leaf

Flickering sunlight and green

A wall of movement.

I smell the wild thyme and sweet grasses

Sun warmed

Aromas mixed with woodland

Leaf mould, decay and sap.

Performance

Under the cool green

A sunbeam stage light

Is switched on

And a host of small flies

Begin to dance.

Meltdown

Hot July day,

Thoughts of the mosses

Under a glassy heat

Wilting grasses

Crackling under stress

Sheep seeking shade

Cattle restless

Marsh Road melted tar.

Cuckoo Pint

Under the hedge

A sunbeam discovers

Seven glowing orange berried

Seed stems.

Herb Paris

Mysterious quadrifolia

Senescent now.

A final flourish

A shiny, round, black seed

Held aloft

An offering

To any creature

That dares to eat it.

Red Berry Folds

Marsh Road, September soft

Red berry folds.

Concealed,watching eyes.

Cattle, pushed on by summer grass,

Alert and mischevious.

Canine adversary barks.

Wren, disturbed, complains.

From deep in the berries

The red berry folds.

Fullsome

Wheat straws

Hanging heavy heads

Full of the issue

Of the land.

Black soil

Wind and rain

Summer heat

Formed into gold.

October Gather

Ripe apples, perfection

With apple-waxed hands

We pick the last of the season

As a lone wasp

Searches near the ground

For imperfection.

Clump

Grass whispers

Here with the old grey ones

Our roots are deep.

Grass whispers

Stillness comes, Linnet's song

Space filled.

King Of The Woods

Calm autumnal morning

Marsh Road

Bright hedges in yellow leaf

And crimson berries

Fiery edges to the lane.

I, overcome, looking to the Moss Wood

Appeal for healing

By Elvish intervention

With Elf medicine.

A wren chitters to me

From the tangle of the bank

I call,

"King of the Woods. Will you ask them

to bless me".

Wren – known as 'King of the Woods'.

Portal

Limestone gate stoops.

White lichen, green moss

Betraying their age.

Guard the passage

The passage of time.

Buried deep in the moss

By bygone men.

They made a gateway

Whereby to exclude

And to retain.

Whereby to release

And to enter.

People, beasts,

Horses, carts and wagons.

Now time has passed

The gateway stoops

Stand guard

But the passage is barred

By rusty, ill-fitting iron.

Worn leaded hangings

Long light of a gate.

Red – berried bryony

Nettle and bramble

Intertwine with corrosion

Wild rose thorns

A fierce reminder

That the way, once open

Is closed.

Beyond the wheat is ripe and sun bleached.

Heavy heads waving

In a wind from the sea.

To the east over the corn

Church bells ring in the village

Remembering those who passed through

The Passage of Time.

Whitbarrow February

A watery window

Appears in the murk

Through the breach

Enters a keen north-easterly.

No respite for those

Cold-necked mountains

Their dales have become

Midnight and brooding.

Snow struggles for brilliance

In absorbent skies

Of prussian blue and deep grey.

In the south

A wallowing body of rain

And mist

Is waiting for wind and tide

To carry it landwards.

Under the advance of the rain

The failing north-easterly

Tears a rift in the cloud.

In the sun shafts

A dull birchen moss wood

Glows purple and white-silver.

Wall – gapping

Foot of the wall

This where the secrets be

Glimpses of others

Their chaos brings insight to me.

Microcosm stalactites

Moon landscape surfaces

After the fall of countless raindrops

Miniature caverns in endless systems.

Dark, insect patrolled world here

Mouse subjects, weasel is King.

Sometimes a discreet mouse cellar

Long forgotten, mummified hazelnuts.

How do snail shells enter here?

Clustered in stone tombs

Returning to the substance they came from

Once moving pebble with life inside.

That scent of earth, leaf, stone,

Damp, sulphurous, unmistakeable

Reassuring in it's continuity

Spiced by the smell of crushed ramsons in Spring

Continuity for me, flat upon flat

Measured time, built this one before.

So often the past accompanies me

In this quiet place beneath the trees.

Estuary

A crossing goods train sounds

Borne on a damp south-westerly

Over hedges and fields

That once belonged to the sea.

Deep foundations in the sands

Metal tracks seem secure

Fine grains shift constantly

Scouring red brick pillars.

Deep channel here now

Last summer a stretch of rippled mud

Now too deep for the Sea Pie

Heron fares well.

Flukes lie here

Mother of pearl and muddy brown

Holding position

While currents tear and churn.

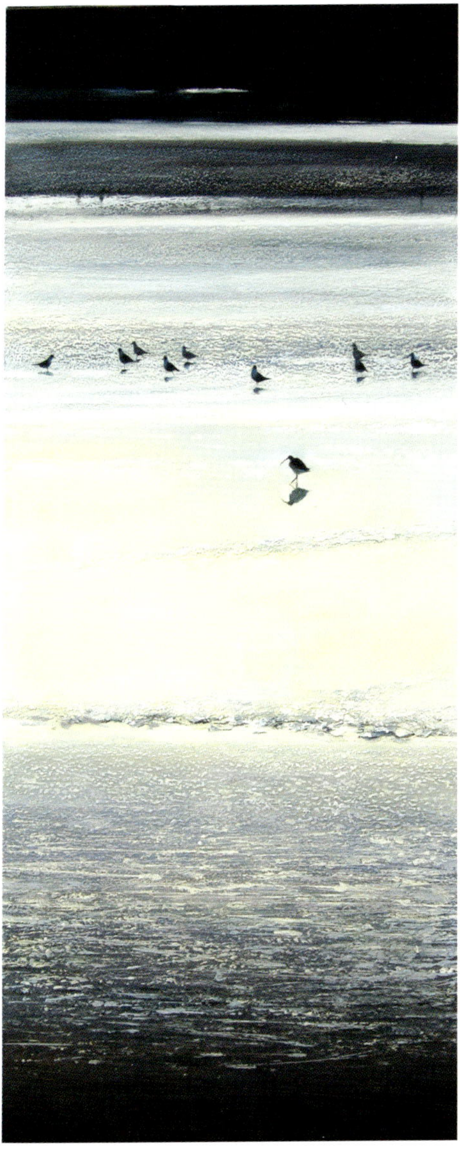

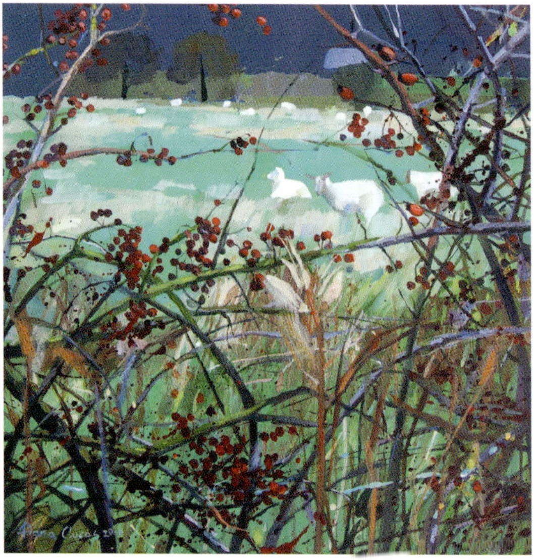

November Quartet

November, ice on dubs

Trees grey

How the rose hips glow red.

                                        Thorn and bramble

                                        Spotted red and orange

Hips and haws   Colours of November.

Colours of November

Splashed on hedges.

                                        Cold blue mountains

                                        Under a November sky

                                        Waiting and waiting

                                        for a white blanket.

Before the storm

Soft breeze this morning

Rising out of the muck hole.

Having crossed sand, mud and snaking channel.

Risen over the banks,

Green bolsters between wild and tamed

Across the sea fields.

Sheep grazing unaware of storm and tide.

December Duo

Distant trees against a cold sunset

Somewhere out there is shelter

Shelter from this north wind.

Winter ash trees on a moss road

Floating, feet always wet

Bodies, ivy clad for warmth.

Voices

Voices in the water

Of the land and it's people

Speaking to me.

Each ripple a story teller

I hear the sounds of voices.

Voices, animal and human.

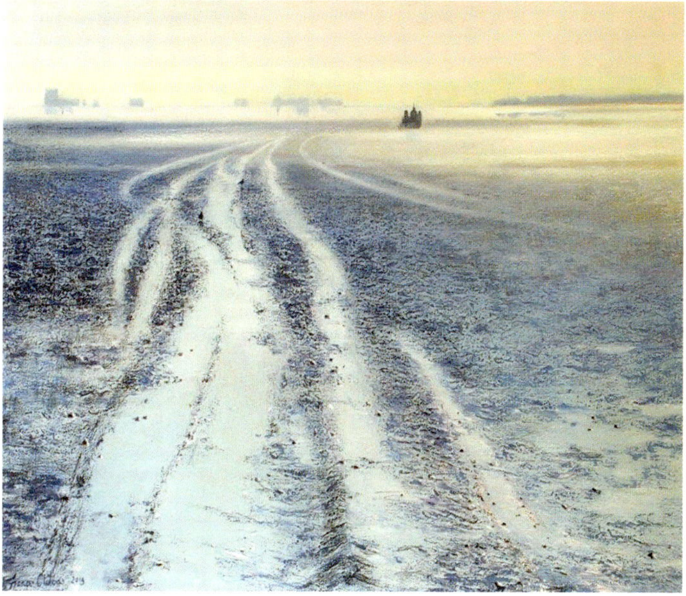

March

Wild March night

She comes with foam flecked mouth

Tearing sand ribs, turning them

Liquid under her feet.

March night with a south-west gale

Sea Pies calling above

Driven from their muddy stances

Resigned to the tidal cycle

Advance and retreat.

Tide

Land melting to sky

Familiar marks have gone

Drops fall on crinkled leaves.

Out there the channels are filling

With the tide surge

The battle between land and sea resumes.

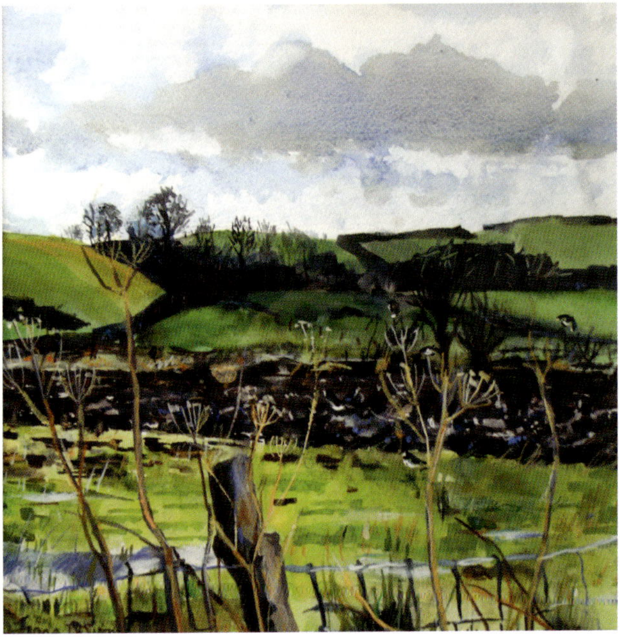

Plough

Bright metal slicing, smacking

Parting lips enter fast and smooth.

Broken root and worm, torn to live

Deliverance of the passage of time.

Smell of newly turned earth

Aroma of straw and wheat

Carried on the wind.

Tatie pickers in the next field

Talk and bent backs.

Swallows swoop as gulls follow the plough.

Flow

Gulls shimmer in call and feather.

The tide is rising

They feel the energy and carry

It into the air above.

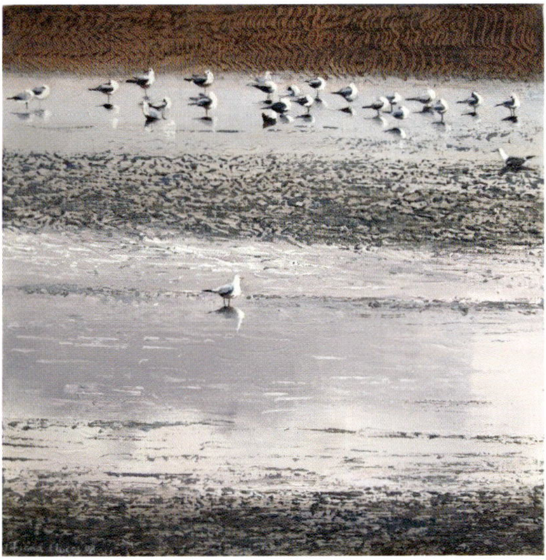

Dissolving Land.

Soft air from the south

Smooth slop of sand cliffs

Falling away in the tide.

Sitting on the bed of an ancient sea

I watch the land dissolve.

After the Shower

Green leaves hanging in water.

Grasses, Campion, Bracken and Bramble.

Soaked,scratched legs and reluctant dog

Just look at that boulder and those gate stoops.

What wonderful work!

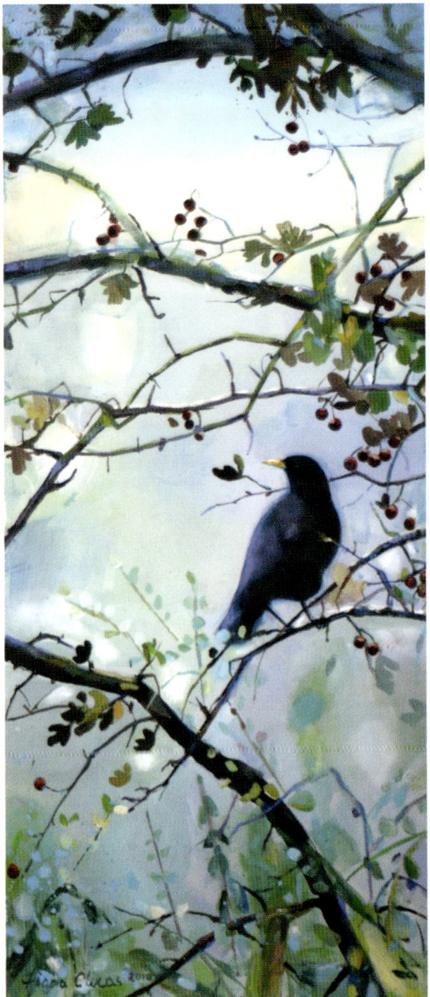

September

Through the swollen red berries, something shone

Like a jewel in the September sun.

I searched.

There was the blackbird's eye returning my gaze

Surface shining bright as a berry skin,

But veneered with something more.

Messages

I hear you wind

As this thorn hedge

Sifts out your rough tongued stories.

Tales from away carried over the restless waters

And the good earth.

The words, the breath of all the living ones

And the traces of the multitudes gone.

There's anger in you today

Tearing at the thorn in frustration.

Snapping leafy limbs from the old ones

Testing the young and supple

As if to break them.

Would you like to rend us too

And hurl us through the sky.

Fulfilment

Red gold seed grass

Yields to the movement of her passing

Swaying, brushing, wafting;

Invisible, intangible.

Her perfume, made of the flowers beckons

Flowers she touches;

Clinging, enlivening, inflaming, releasing, soporific.

That faintest stir among the stems.

Deep within the sward

Even the smallest feel her presence.

This evening she walks

Beneath the rising moon

Promise of harvest to come.

Walking the Marsh Road

Fresh wind from the sea

Catching that peculiar salt smell.

Here on land, the air is full

Full of the scents of summer

Meadowsweet and Cranesbill.

Grasses bending, heavy with seed

Gulls resting, in the mown fields.

A flick of the wing

Off they rise, over the banks

To settle on the marsh,

Waiting for tide to ebb

To search for easy pickings

On the mud.

Left there by their salty provider.

Snowy Anthills, Sizergh Fell

The old ones pillows are scattered

Full and round in the setting sun

Blue shadows and pink glow

Stillness and softness under the cool white sheet.

Attitude

Raven crossing the hardland from the north – west

Over the nests of man

Pouring down scorn in passing

Away to the far moss.

Moss Road

Walking the moss road, wild wet morning

A shovel full of grain scattered

On the shiny, wet surface

Shaken and lost on the bumpy road home.

" So they must have harvested the last field".

Now, far out along the flood bank

Where black sloes sway on leafless branches

Ragtag crows feeding in the wet, rutted field

Spilt seeds, short lived pickings as the days draw in.

A raven crosses high before me

Composed flight, despite the gale.

Scorns the gleaning brotherhood below him

Away to the fell where he holds a secret.

Old Road – October

A clear yellow leaf lay at the roadside.

Glowing like the sun of the past summer

As if a curtain had been opened

In the leafy mass that it lay on.

The wind raised it up,

And another window opened

On the surface of a puddle.

Christmas Time, Heversham Marsh

The wind, tonight, has crossed the mosses

North – west, cold and sleaty.

Feel it sting the face

Carrying off the warmth of home.

Tearfully I face the storm

Tears from cold with heart – tears of warmth

Old friend, reality, at last.

Shades have been over me for so long

Wind stirs memories, slapping on the senses.

All around is the constant play of life.

Here, it feels like the centre

Dark, low and bleak.

Constant as the tide over the bank.

Wading birds pass overhead to feed

Darkness hiding them.

Even by the light of a full fleeting moon.

Life Support

This land is a sponge

Rain falling,clinging, sinking,

Soaking, swelling, dripping from one to another.

Defying gravity, slipping, sliding, drifting, steaming,

Eventually settling on the living.

Living are everywhere

Teeming, solitary, green, grey, red, rough, smooth,

Spiky, simple and complex.

On the ground, off the ground,

On objects stuck in the ground,

On rocks, trees, trees on trees.

Open to the light, exposed to all,

Or in deep, dark recesses, hidden and mysterious.

And as the rain falls, the sponge swells to meet the sky.

Where they meet miracles happen.

July, Sizergh Fell

Hand shielding the eyes in bright sunshine

A bird rises from behind those anthills

Striving for distance

A shower of glinting, floating hawkbit seeds

Silent, soft explosion,

Sparked by the woodpecker's wing.

Plain Road

Sticky melted tar

Sucking at the feet

The road disappears

Vanishing in a haze.

Cattle and sheep are still

Seeking shade however meagre

Flies frustrate

Tails swish, heads toss.

Clegs rise casually

Landing sleepily

Gold flecked eyes, impartial gaze

Any blood will suffice.

Perfume of dried grass

Cut fields surround

A net of dark hedges

Marks out bleached meadows.

A crow drifts over

Looking for mower – chopped mice

Alerts the lapwings

They rise through habit, not fear.

If only I was only an inch or so

Lush verges look so inviting

Cool shade, flowery smells

Herbaceous trunks towering above me.

Living with the Artist

Delivered to the seascape, I wait, not for long

The engagement has already begun.

"I'm just getting out" you say.

"Alright I'll wait here".

"I'll just be a minute. Is that alright?"

"Of course it is" I say.

I wait for the parting ritual to be completed.

I watch you as you walk towards the cliff edge.

You sink to the ground and immediacy begins.

Rising and focussed, then forging onwards.

Face raised to the light, a receiver of the world.

I see the energy building, walk receive, walk accept.

Until you are just a tiny figure on the headland.

Absorption having led you astray.

You retrace your steps, slower now.

The animal in your soul has been fed.

As you pick up paper and paints,

The digestion process begins.

Out of season

Thrush in the crown

Of a bare grey ash tree

Song so much the sweeter

It being a December dusk.

Travellers

Solway bound Pinkfeet

High, in bright sunlight

Glinting on hard feather.

I watch, envious of their freedom.

Illumination

Four swans rising

White light,

On this rainy

October day.

Whitbarrow gift

Sun shower out of Pether Pots

Dropping through the hazel groves

Crossing the moss

Building a rainbow

From Toll Bar to Sim Well.

Summer's End

Faint feeling of change

North – easterly from Whinfell way.

Even so the mauve scabious blurr

Still swallows from view fleeing rabbits.

The Fell smells of Autumn

Mixture of decay, animals and fruits

The soil is beginning to slumber

Resting from Summer's work.

I sense a sigh from the land

Ready to sleep, a resignation,

Acceptance, a fulfillment.

Another breath of cool air

Carries a waft of land smell.

Sweet flower perfumes are fading

Cold, damp earth absorbs them.